HEAT AND ENERGY

Design	Cooper · West
Editor	Margaret Fagan
Researcher	Cecilia Weston-Baker
Illustrator	Louise Nevett

Consultant | J. W. Warren Ph.D.
Formerly reader in Physics
Education, Department of
Physics, Brunel University, London.

This edition published
in 1990 by
Franklin Watts
96 Leonard St
London EC2A 4RH

Designed and produced by
Aladdin Books Ltd
70 Old Compton Street
London W1

ISBN 0 86313 382 7 (hardback)

ISBN 0 7496 0380 1 (paperback)

Printed in Belgium

SIMPLY SCIENCE

HEAT AND ENERGY

Kathryn Whyman

FRANKLIN WATTS
London · New York · Toronto · Sydney

INTRODUCTION

Everything we do needs energy. Running, cycling, walking, reading a book, or even sleeping – all these actions use energy. We need energy to heat our homes; a jet plane needs energy to push it through the air; a train needs energy to pull its carriages along the tracks.

Energy is constantly changing from one form to another. Heat is a way of moving energy from place to place. In this book you will find out what heat and energy are and where the energy on our Earth comes from.

CONTENTS

WHAT IS ENERGY?

You will have heard the word "energy" many times before. Sometimes people use it to describe how they feel. Someone who feels tired may say "I've no energy today".

But in science "energy" has a special meaning. It is not something we can see or feel. It is a measure of how much "work" can be done. Whenever we push or pull something that moves, we are doing work. And when we do work we use energy. You use energy when you push open a door or pull on your clothes. Some activities, such as running, use a great deal of energy.

Machines also do work. The mechanical digger in the photograph can move big piles of earth and rubble. It gets its energy from the oil and oxygen burned in its engine.

Whenever your body moves you use energy

A mechanical digger at work, moving earth into a dump truck

Harvesting a crop ripened by the Sun

THE ENERGY CYCLE

All the energy on our Earth comes from the Sun! But before we can use the energy from the Sun, it usually has to go through many changes. And often when energy changes it is moved, or "transferred", from place to place. How does the energy we need to run, bicycle or swim, reach our bodies from the Sun?

Every time we eat vegetables and fruit, energy is made available to our bodies. The energy comes from the chemicals which make up these foods. Bread, an important food in many parts of the world, is also made from a plant – wheat. Where does the energy in wheat come from?

Energy from the Sun makes wheat grow. With sunlight, the wheat can combine water from the soil and carbon dioxide from the air to make chemicals which eventually end up in our bread. This transfer of energy from one place to another is all part of the energy cycle. Even the energy we get from meat originally came from the Sun as the animals from which we get the meat ate plants.

The food chain

Wheat takes up water through its roots. Its leaves absorb carbon dioxide. In sunlight the wheat can turn these simple ingredients into sugar, starch and oxygen (a process called photosynthesis). Sugar and starch may either be stored in the grain or used to make the plant grow. The food in the plant is passed on when an animal eats it. This transfer of energy from the Sun to animals, via plants and oxygen, is called a "food chain".

ENERGY CHANGES

Sometimes it may seem as if energy is "lost" or "used up". But in fact energy is *never* made or destroyed – it just changes from one form to another, or is moved from one place to another.

We have already seen how energy from the Sun can be transferred to our food. But the Sun's energy may change in other ways too.

When the Sun shines, some parts of the air get warmer than others. The warmer air rises and the cooler air rushes in to take its place. This moving air current is called wind. Wind is a source of energy and can be made to do useful work. For example, it can be used to move the sails of a windmill. The moving sails can also do work. In the photograph, they are turning parts of a machine to pump up water to irrigate the land.

Sound

When you hit a drum, the energy of the falling drumstick is transferred to the drum skin. The skin moves up and down (or vibrates). Peas placed on the surface of the drum show this clearly. The energy of the drum skin is, in turn, transferred to the air to make sound.

Energy from the wind drives the sails of a windpump

POTENTIAL AND KINETIC ENERGY

Imagine you are holding a weight above your head. The weight may not seem to have any energy. But when you drop the weight it can do work. For example, it might make a dent in the floor. If the weight does work, it must have energy.

Before it falls, we say that the weight has "potential energy". As it falls it gets closer and closer to the ground and has less and less potential energy. But we know that energy is never lost – so where has the potential energy gone? It has changed into the movement, or "kinetic energy", of the falling weight.

An archer preparing to shoot an arrow does work on the bow to make it bend. The bow now has potential energy because of its new shape. As soon as the archer lets go of the bowstring this potential energy is released. It is transferred to the arrow, giving it kinetic energy.

Cog wheel — Spring wound up — Key — Spring unwinds

Springs

Springs can be made to do work. The diagram shows how a spring in a clockwork car is wound up when the key is turned. The spring has now been given potential energy. As the spring unwinds its potential energy is released and it provides kinetic energy for the turning wheels.

The archer creates potential energy by pulling the bowstring

BURNING

Another example of an energy change occurs when a substance catches fire and burns. You can make a fire by rubbing two dry sticks together. The work you do on the sticks provides them with energy and makes them hotter. Eventually, they will catch fire, or ignite. As it is very awkward to start a fire in this way, we usually use matches. The head of the match contains special chemicals. When the match is "struck" against sandpaper, the chemicals get hot and ignite.

With oxygen

Without oxygen

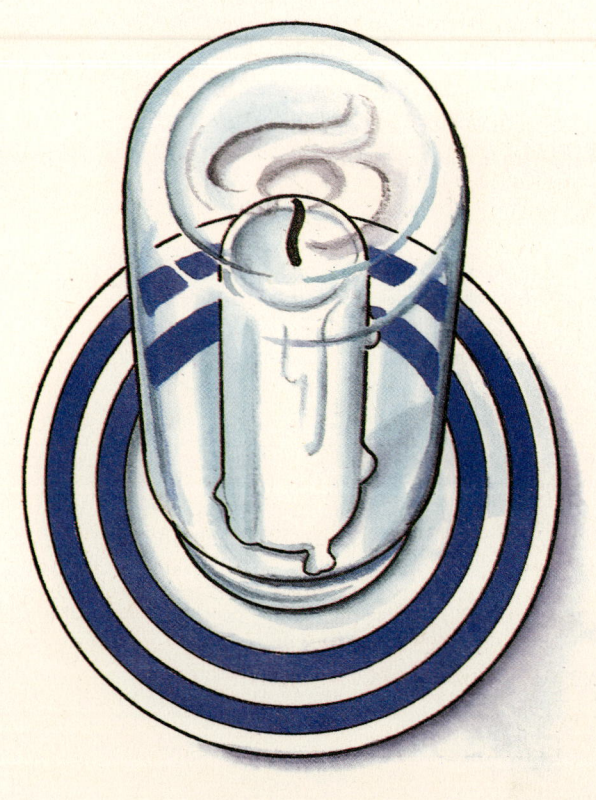

Things cannot burn without oxygen. Air contains oxygen and the wax of a candle uses some of this oxygen as it burns. If a jam jar is placed over the burning candle the flame soon flickers and goes out. Once all the oxygen in the jar has been used the candle can no longer keep alight.

When a substance burns energy changes and is *transferred* as heat. The substance itself also changes and cannot be changed back again. This type of change is said to be "irreversible". Fire, therefore, as well as being useful can be destructive; it can destroy buildings, damage forests and kill living things. Since fires need high temperatures and oxygen to keep them burning removing either of these can put a fire out. Other materials, such as sand can also be used to smother a fire and dampen the flames.

Foam is also used to put out a fire by depriving it of oxygen

FUELS

A fuel is something which releases energy as it burns with oxygen. Coal, oil and gas are fuels which come from the remains of dead plants and animals and are called "fossil fuels". Fossil fuels took millions of years to form and cannot be replaced once they have been used up. You will remember that energy from the Sun is transferred to plants as they grow. Coal is formed from dead plants. When it is burned some of the Sun's energy is released again as heat.

Oil is a very valuable fuel. Found deep under the Earth's surface, crude oil is a thick, black liquid which is refined before it is used. Many fuels can be produced from crude oil: petrol for cars, for example, or aviation fuel for aeroplanes. Today, substances which can provide nuclear energy, such as uranium, are also used as fuels.

A short history of oil

1. Millions of years ago tiny plants and animals, different from those which exist today, lived in the sea. Sunlight, water and minerals allowed the plants to make chemicals. The animals fed on these plants.

2. When they died, the plants and animals sank to the sea bed. There they became trapped by layers of silt and sand.

3. The silt and sand slowly changed into rocks which pushed hard on the remains of the animals and plants. Buried deep underground these remains became very hot and eventually turned into oil or gas.

1
Silt and sand

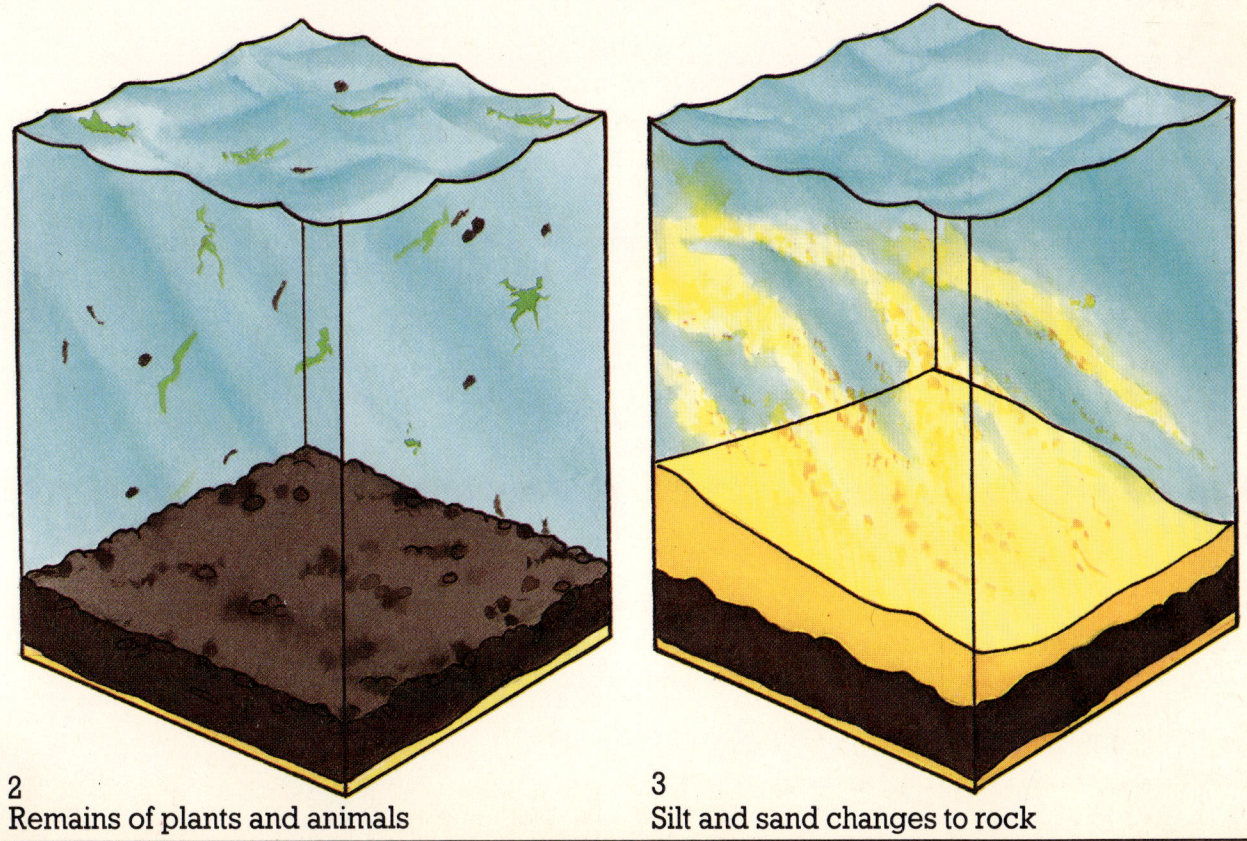

Oil rigs drill deep under the ocean bed

2
Remains of plants and animals

3
Silt and sand changes to rock

HEAT

Heat is a way of moving or transferring energy from place to place. Heat always transfers energy from a warmer place to somewhere cooler. For example, the energy in a hot drink moves from the drink to the cooler air surrounding it.

Heat can travel in three different ways. When the land warms the air above, the air rises and this upward movement forces cooler air to take its place. Heat is being transferred from one place to another by the moving air. This type of heat transfer which takes place in both gases and liquids is called "convection". Rising currents of warm air help a glider stay up in the air longer. In a solid, however, heat is transferred from the hottest point, along the solid, to the coolest point. This is called "conduction". Heat from the Sun reaches us by travelling across space by "radiation".

Convection
Water at the bottom of the pan gets hot first and rises. The arrows show how the water forms a "convection current".

Conduction
If heat is transferred to one part of a knife from a source, it will spread out along the metal blade in both directions.

Radiation
Heat travels from a bar fire mostly by radiation. Energy is transferred as a "ray" which spreads out in all directions.

Hot air rises by convection; heat transferred by conduction melts metal

The Sun's rays warm us by radiation

TEMPERATURE

We often want to know exactly how hot or cold something is. We call this its "temperature". The temperature of our bodies is 37°C (98.6°F), except when we are ill. Even though the air around us is often cooler or warmer than 37°C (98.6°F), our bodies have ways of staying at the same temperature. This is not true of all animals, such as reptiles and fish. A lizard's body temperature may vary depending on its surroundings.

Materials are affected by temperature. Many substances can exist in three different forms; as a solid, liquid or gas. When water freezes at 0°C (−32°F) it forms ice, a solid. If water is heated to 100°C (212°F) it will boil and quickly form water vapour, a gas.

Our skin can feel whether something is hot or cold but it cannot take accurate temperatures. Different parts of your skin may even give you different information about the same bowl of water as in the example below.

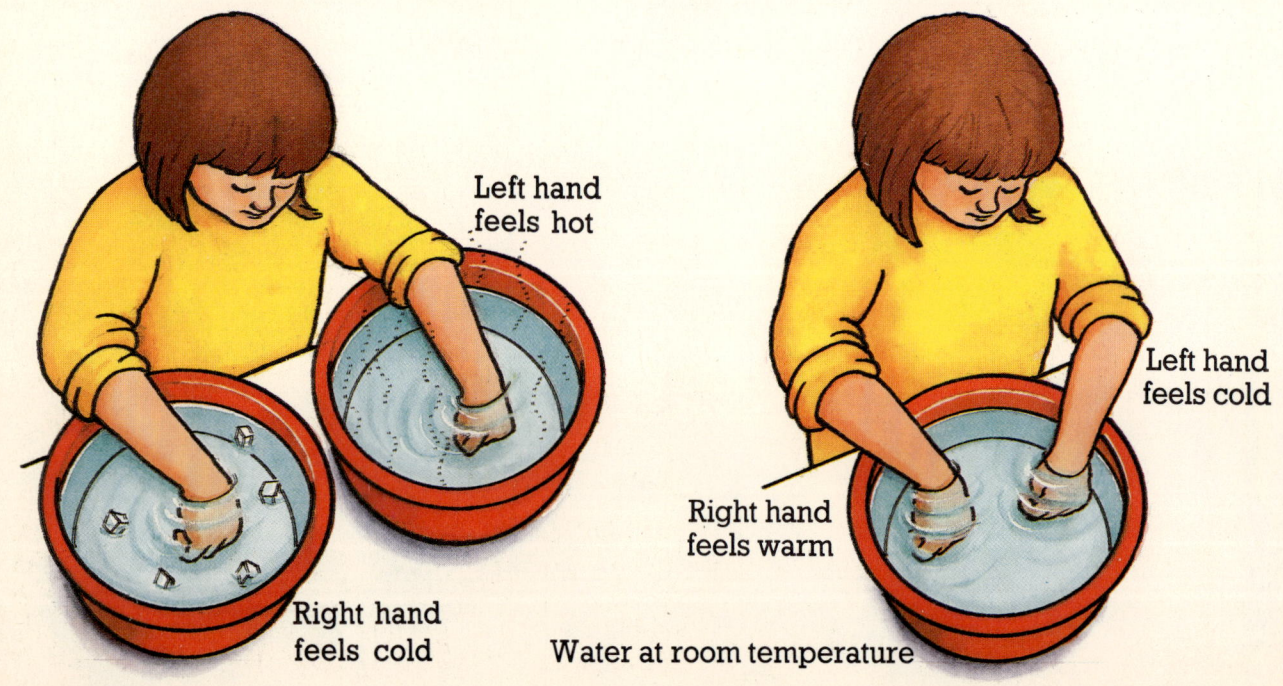

Left hand feels hot

Right hand feels cold

Left hand feels cold

Right hand feels warm

Water at room temperature

100°C (212°F) Water boils

Temperature can be measured using a thermometer. This thermometer is made of glass and has a narrow tube running through it. The tube opens into a bulb which is filled with mercury, a liquid metal. The hotter it gets the more the mercury expands and moves up the tube. The glass has a scale printed on it. The level the mercury reaches in melting ice is called 0 degrees centigrade (C) (−32 degrees Fahrenheit (F)) and the level it expands to in boiling water is called 100°C (212°F). The "geyser" (above) occurs because water running deep in the Earth boils and is forced to the surface. Icebergs (below) occur where temperature is below 0°C (−32°F).

0°C (−32°F) Ice melts

EXPANSION AND CONTRACTION

If you have ever had difficulty unscrewing a tight bottle top you may have found that running hot water over the top made it unscrew easily. The reason for this is that things get a little bigger when they get hot. We say they "expand".

Metals expand more than many other materials. It is very important for engineers to remember this when they design bridges. During a hot summer, the metal parts of a bridge expand. To stop it buckling, small gaps are left in the bridge when it is built. Railway lines also expand in hot weather.

If a metal is cooled it will get smaller, or "contract". Telegraph wires are always hung loosely so that in winter, when they contract and become tighter, they do not snap.

Thermostat

Thermostats are used to control the temperature of an appliance, an oven, for example. Gas passes through a valve into the oven where it is burned. As the oven gets hot, the brass tube of the thermostat attached to the valve expands. This pulls the valve in and reduces the flow of gas. When the oven cools down, the brass tube contracts. This causes the valve to open fully again and allows more gas to enter the oven.

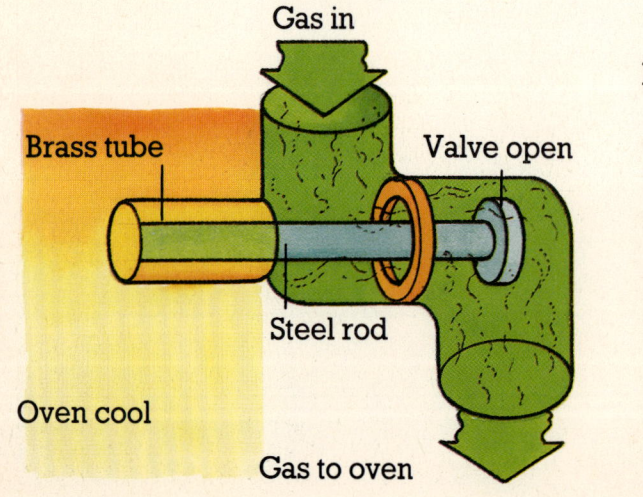

Gas in

Brass tube

Valve open

Steel rod

Oven cool

Gas to oven

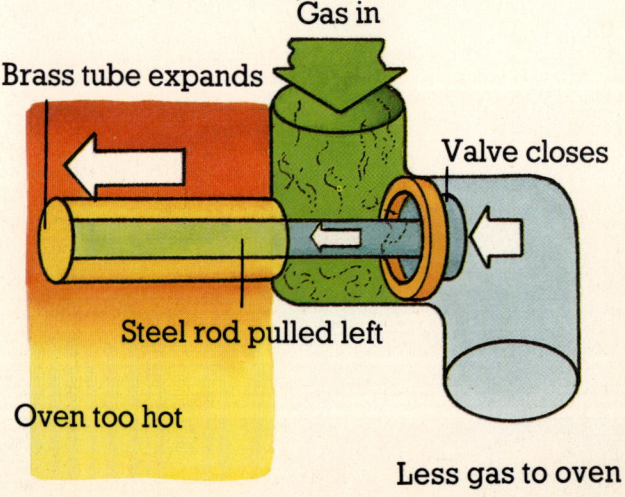

Gas in

Brass tube expands

Valve closes

Steel rod pulled left

Oven too hot

Less gas to oven

23

A bridge is built with small gaps between each section so it can expand in hot weather

INSULATORS AND CONDUCTORS

Heat can travel quickly through some substances. These are called "conductors" and include metals such as copper. Copper feels cold when you touch it because it conducts heat away from your body. Other substances, for example wood and plastic, carry heat more slowly and so feel warmer. These are called "insulators".

Air is a good insulator and woollen clothes, which contain lots of air spaces, keep us warm. Mammals living in cold climates often have thick fur which traps a layer of insulating air around them. Some, such as seals, also have a layer of fat (blubber) to insulate them in water.

An elephant, however, needs to keep cool. Its big ears provide a large area through which heat can leave its body.

Vacuum flask

A vacuum flask keeps hot things hot (or cold things cold). The two silvered walls have a vacuum between them. A vacuum insulates since heat can only travel across it by radiation. The shiny surfaces of the flask absorb little heat, so any heat is reflected backwards and forwards between them. A cork stopper provides insulation at the top of the flask.

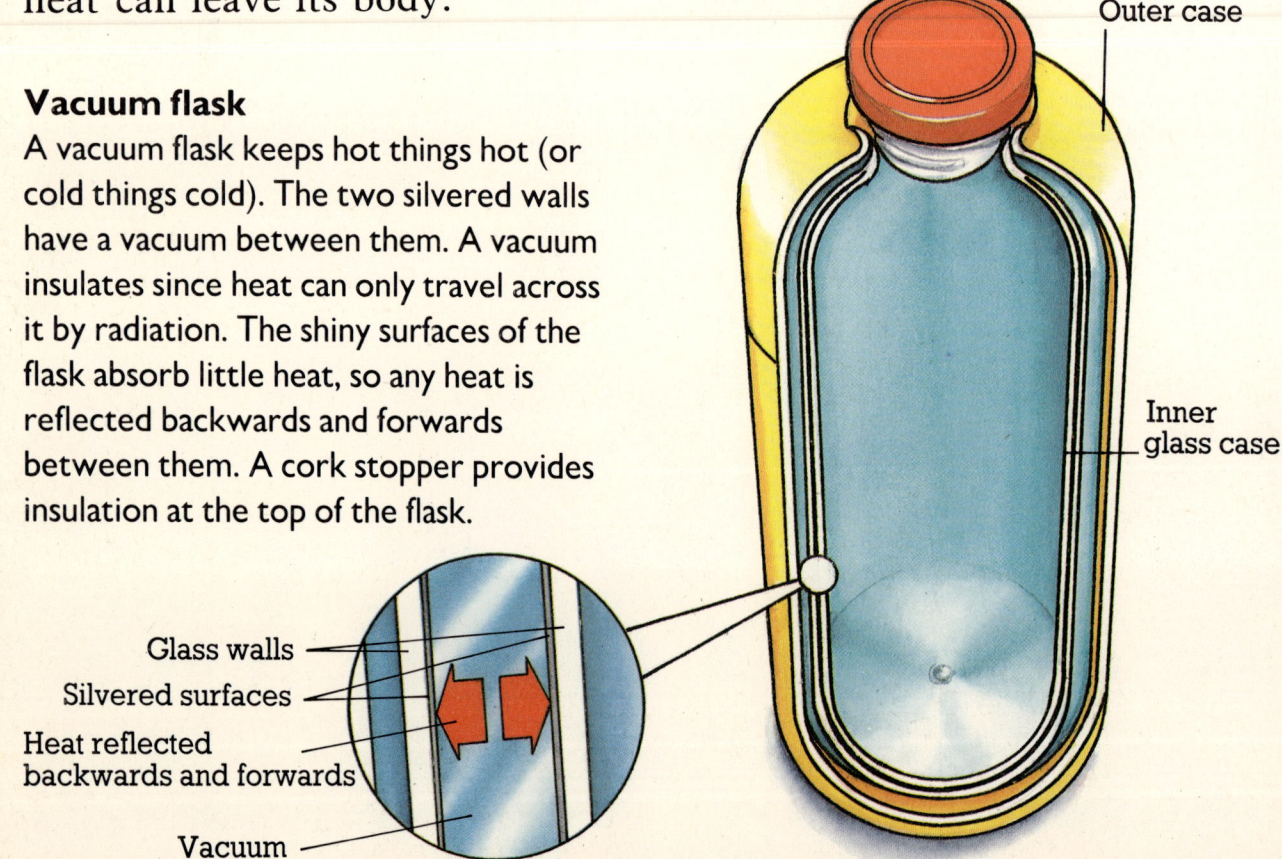

Outer case

Inner glass case

Glass walls

Silvered surfaces

Heat reflected backwards and forwards

Vacuum

Keeping cool and keeping warm; all mammals need to control their body temperature

HEAT AND ENERGY IN THE HOME

Energy is used in our homes in many forms. Our lights and heating, our cookers and fridges and other appliances all depend on energy. Most homes use electricity or gas to transfer energy to an appliance so that it can do work. However, other fuels such as coal and wood are still used in some parts of the world to provide heat and light.

In cold climates, heat is always moving from the house to the colder air outside. Houses like the one in the diagram use a variety of insulators to cut down heat transfer.

In hot countries, houses have to keep out the Sun's heat. They have thick, solid walls to insulate them and shutters to keep out the sunlight during the hottest time of the day.

Painting buildings white helps to keep out the Sun's heat

The house is supplied with gas, water and electricity by underground pipes and sewage is piped out (1). Some gas is burned with oxygen in a boiler (2) to provide hot water which is stored in an insulated tank (3). Hot water is also used to fill radiators (4). More gas may be burned in a gas oven (5). Electricity is used to provide light (6). The family car is driven by petrol which burns in its engine (7). Gaps in the wall (8) and between double-glazed windows (9) trap air. The loft is lagged for insulation (10) and a duvet (11) provides insulation in bed.

MAKE YOUR OWN WINDMILL

A windmill allows us to use energy from the
wind. This one can use movement of air to work
the sails and so cause the movement of a hammer.
You will need to use a hair dryer or fan heater as
a source of "wind" to drive your windmill.

What you need
A clean empty milk or fruit juice carton
Cardboard
Two plastic biro insides
Two thick straws
Scissors

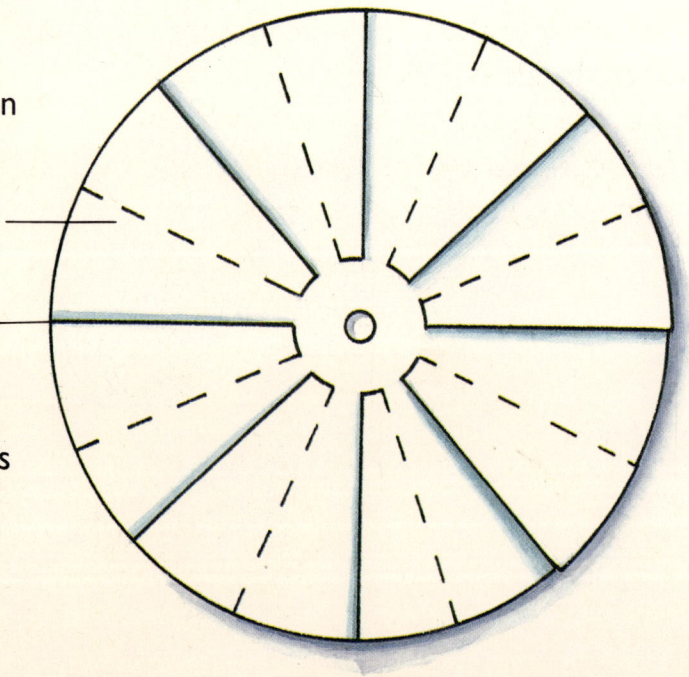

To make the sails, mark out a circle of
card as shown. Cut along the solid lines
and fold along the dotted ones. The
carton will become the windmill's
tower. Make a sloping roof from
cardboard and paint it if you like.

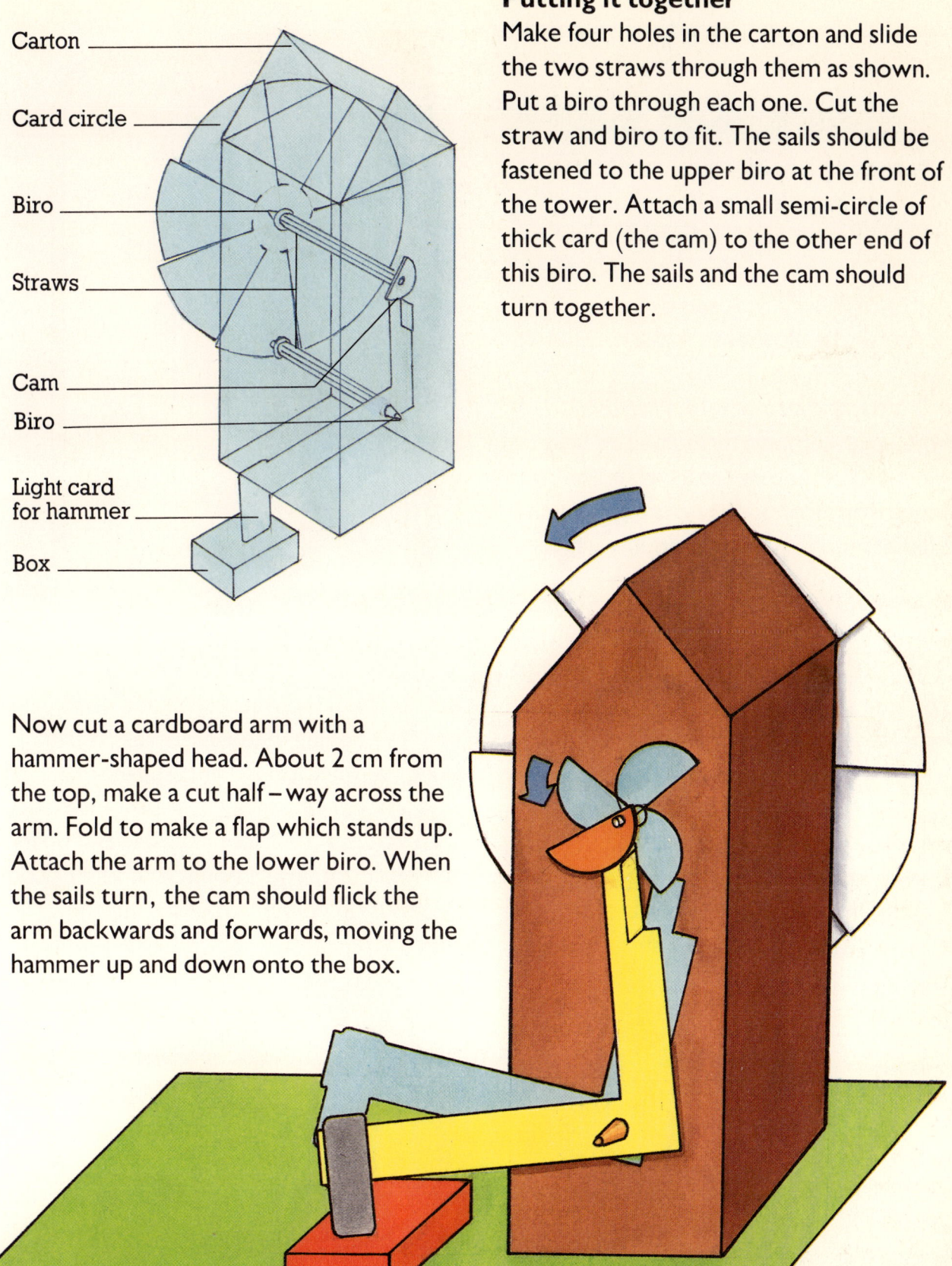

Carton

Card circle

Biro

Straws

Cam
Biro

Light card
for hammer

Box

Putting it together

Make four holes in the carton and slide the two straws through them as shown. Put a biro through each one. Cut the straw and biro to fit. The sails should be fastened to the upper biro at the front of the tower. Attach a small semi-circle of thick card (the cam) to the other end of this biro. The sails and the cam should turn together.

Now cut a cardboard arm with a hammer-shaped head. About 2 cm from the top, make a cut half – way across the arm. Fold to make a flap which stands up. Attach the arm to the lower biro. When the sails turn, the cam should flick the arm backwards and forwards, moving the hammer up and down onto the box.

Alcohol and mercury thermometers

We use many different types of thermometers at home, in hospitals and in laboratories. In colder countries where temperatures are often below 0°C, many outdoor or household thermometers are filled with alcohol. Alcohol has a lower freezing point than water or mercury. A red dye is usually added to the alcohol to make it easier to see.

Mercury thermometers are used when high temperatures need to be measured. Mercury has a higher boiling point than alcohol. Doctors use a special kind of mercury thermometer called a clinical thermometer.

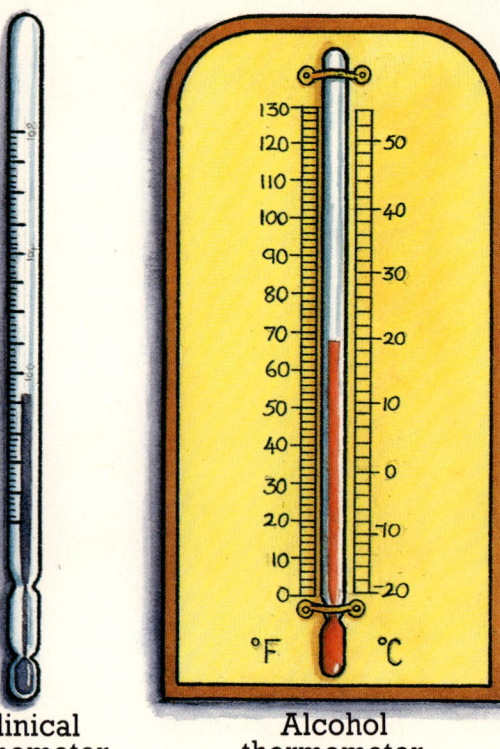

Clinical thermometer

Alcohol thermometer

The difference between energy and temperature

Imagine a blacksmith holding a red-hot nail by a pair of pliers and dipping it into a bowl of cold water. The temperature of the water would hardly change. However, if a kettle of boiling water is poured into a bowl of cold water, the temperature of the cold water rises. This is because there is more *energy* in a kettle of boiling water than in a red-hot nail. Yet boiling water has a very much lower temperature than a red-hot nail. The amount of energy in a substance such as a nail, does not only depend on its temperature. The amount of energy also depends on how much of the substance there is.

GLOSSARY

Appliance
A piece of equipment which has a particular purpose, for example, a hair dryer.

Cam
A bit of a machine. It may change circular movement of one part of a machine into up and down movement of another part.

Carbon dioxide
A gas. A small amount of this is in the air.

Double-glazed
Describes windows made with two panes of glass with a gap between them.

Energy
Something which can do work uses energy.

Heat
A process in which energy is transferred from one place to another.

Irrigate
Supply agricultural land with water.

Lagged
Covered in insulating material (that is, material which conducts heat poorly).

Minerals
Chemicals found in the earth. Several, such as magnesium, are necessary for plants to grow properly.

Photosynthesis
A process in which green plants use the energy of sunlight to make sugars from water and carbon dioxide.

Refined
Separated and purified.

Silt
Mud which has been deposited by water.

Vacuum
Space in which there is nothing, not even air.

Valve
A device which can control the movement of a gas or a liquid, often through a pipe. It usually only allows movement in one direction.

Vibrates
Moves quickly to and fro.

Work
When a force is exerted on something which moves, we say that work has been done.

INDEX

Photographic Credits:
Cover, contents page and pages 7, 8, 13, 19 (2), 21, 23, 25 (inset) and 26, Tony Stone Associates; title page and pages 19 and 21, Susan Griggs Agency; page 6, Allsport; page 11, Peter Fraenkel; page 15, Zefa; page 17, Spectrum; page 25, Survival Anglia; page 28, Cooper–West.

PRINTED IN BELGIUM BY

proost
INTERNATIONAL BOOK PRODUCTION